MAGIC DRAFTING

MAGIC DRAFTING

Gabriella Kovac

Kangaroo Press

© Gabriella Kovac 1992, 1994

This edition published in 1994 by Kangaroo Press Pty Ltd
3 Whitehall Road Kenthurst NSW 2156 Australia
P.O. Box 6125 Dural Delivery Centre NSW 2158
Typeset by G.T. Setters Pty Limited
Printed in Hong Kong through Colorcraft Ltd

ISBN 0 86417 609 0

Contents

Introduction

I have written this book for those who want to have fun and are not scared of trying something new, and because I wanted to simplify the art of making clothes.

The book contains step by step instructions for creating basic garments to fit all body shapes—fat, thin, out of proportion and just ordinary.

It seems to me that I have been designing and making patterns all my life, starting as a small child with making doll's clothes.

My parents migrated from Hungary to Australia and started manufacturing ladies' garments. This was a great opportunity for me to create, design and help my parents. I soon learned that all body shapes were different and that the technically correct pattern did not fit real life bodies. Eventually I worked out a way to get garments to look good and actually fit the bodies of my clients.

As time progressed I worked in the fashion industry and started my own business in individually knitted garments. I found that the original concept I started to use as a young girl was still the most workable system I had come across.

I started to teach my system five years ago and was amazed to find the number of false and complicated systems in the subject of fashion and design. I find it the simplest method to use for all sorts of clothing and fabrics—from knitwear to silks and gaberdines, for men, women and children.

There is a distinct difference between the subject of mathematics and the artistic shape of the human body.

The best way to thwart talented designers is to load them down with maths. This practice has taken away the initiative of thousands of young designers and home sewers. If a commercial pattern they have bought doesn't fit, they don't dare cut the pattern or alter it. With my method, altering patterns will be done with confidence and mistakes can just become new designs.

To me, making someone a dress should be fun and an adventure, not hard work. Our bodies are not accurate or made from one mould. The human body is a soft rounded shape and we are all individual, not one being the same as another. The body doesn't conform to exact geometric rules and regulations. And the left side is rarely the mirror image of the right (or vice versa).

This book is especially for the home dressmaker and creative designers who love the art form of creating new garments without the encumbrance of mathematics. It will outline the few rules you will need to know for accuracy in achieving this aim (or product). There won't be a need for brilliance in maths.

I would like to thank all those friends who helped in the making of this book—in particular, Peter Shead, Albert McGraw, my husband John, Roderick for technical drawings, Keith Chessell for computer graphics and Jodey Wills for layout and design.

My wish is that you will use this book and come to love sewing and designing as much as I do. Good luck and happy sewing.

How to Use this Book

My main purpose in writing this book is to pass on the knowledge I have gained in the last thirty years. Some of you will have previous knowledge in pattern-making and others are just embarking on the journey. To be sure you obtain the most benefit from my book I am going to deal with each chapter individually so you can choose where you want to start from.

The picture blocks below represent the stepping stones to gaining the knowledge from the first to last chapter.

Chapter 1 deals with the skirt. If you follow the diagrams from left to right you will learn:

How to take individual measurements to create the well fitting skirt
To place those measurements on paper
How to fit your garment; and
Have your individual skirt pattern

Chapters 2 to 6 are the most important chapters, as they deal with the bodice created from your own measurements.

It merges the art of dressmaking with the art of pattern-making and is shown in step by step form.

When you fully understand making the bodice, you will have the knowledge to make professional garments for the most discerning person as well as the ability to alter your commercial patterns.

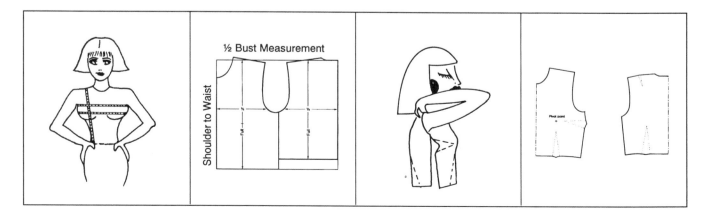

7

Chapter 7, The Sleeves, will instruct you on creating a perfect bell shape for your sleeve head, step by step.

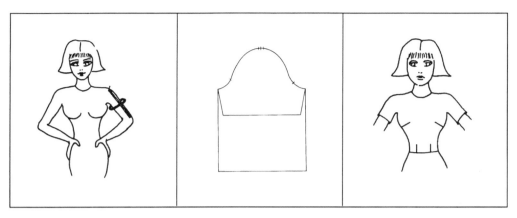

Chapter 8, Creating Collars, will teach you how to design and create most collar designs. This is done by showing you the relationship between them.

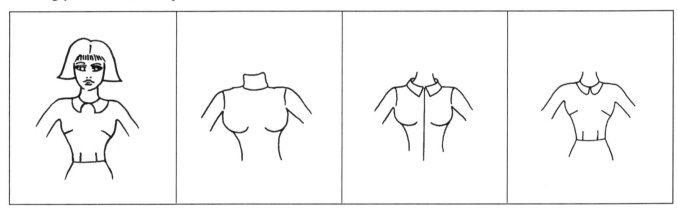

Chapters 9 to 17 give you some ideal garments to create, so you can gain confidence in your designs and the use of this book.

Chapter 18 deals with sewing instructions in general terms. I felt that for this book, these instructions were ample. However, later books will contain specific sewing instructions for each garment.

Materials

Now, are you all ready to start? You will need some tools before you begin—paper to draw on, sticky tape, pins, tape measure, calico, pencils, marking pen, scissors, and the most important of all, a flexible ruler or grading ruler.

This ruler is so important that I am giving you instructions on how to use it. If you can't find or buy one, it can be substituted by a flexible plastic and an ordinary ruler, but this is a lot harder. (See Drafting Supplies on page 79.)

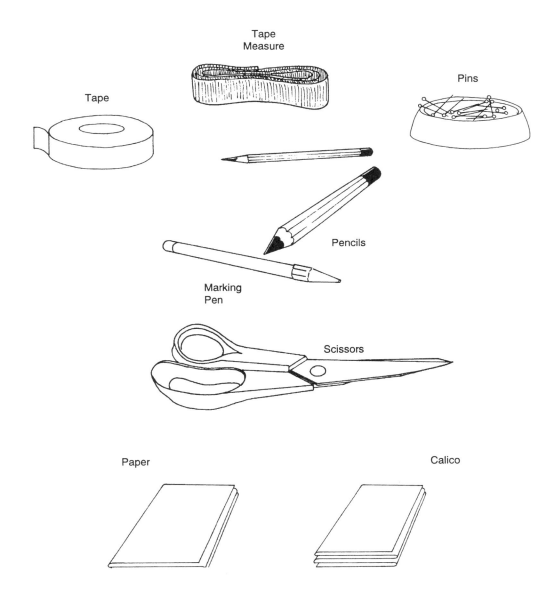

Tape Measure

Tape

Pins

Pencils

Marking Pen

Scissors

Paper

Calico

The Use of the Flexible Ruler

In my thirty years experience as a pattern maker/designer I have found the flexible ruler is totally indispensable. With this ruler, pattern makers can make their basic garments in different sizes, from a size 10 to a 12, 14 or 16. This is the only tool used for shaping and redesigning the lines in the garments.

By looking at the following diagrams, you will get an idea of how to use it, and by the time you finish the book you will become an expert in its use. See Drafting Supplies (page 79) for information on where to obtain the ruler, paper and other materials.

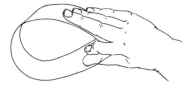 The ruler will fully curve held by index and thumb on one end and remaining three fingers on the other end as shown here.

 By having the ruler sitting in your palm and exerting pressure from both sides, a U-shape can be formed suitable for your neck curve and the main curve at the armhole.

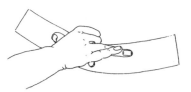 By holding the ruler in between your index and middle finger, and exerting pressure with your ring finger and thumb from the other side of the ruler, you will get a slight curve suitable for hip line and slight curves at the armhole.

You can use the horizontal line grid on your ruler to draw different size parallel lines using the line on the ruler as a guide.

New body measurements are obtained by using curved ruler and connecting new lines.

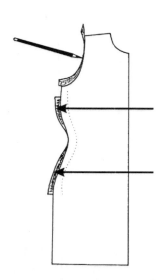

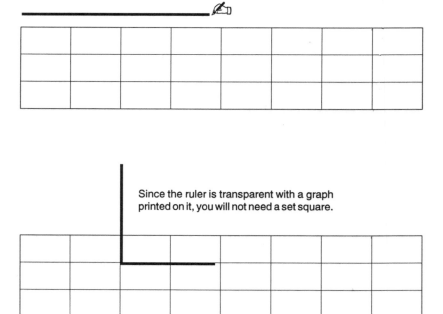

Since the ruler is transparent with a graph printed on it, you will not need a set square.

Once you have obtained all the materials necessary for using this book—we can start!

CHAPTER 1
Creating the Skirt

In this first chapter let us start with your skirt. At the end of this chapter you will master the ability to create your own skirt. This will fit and look better than any skirt you have previously made or bought. So let us look at the first step:

Diagram 1

Make sure you get enough paper in length and width to cut a full skirt, approximately 120 cm × 70 cm (47" × 27½"). Fold the paper in half lengthways.

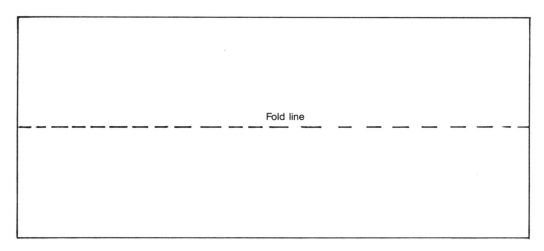

Fold line

Diagram 2

Approximately 5 cm (2") from the top end of your paper draw a line at right angles to the fold. This indicates the waistline.

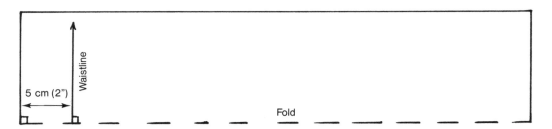

5 cm (2")

Waistline

Fold

Diagram 3

Now from your waist, measure down to the start of your hip curve, i.e. top hip bone. This will be approximately 9 cm (3½") down. Draw a corresponding line across the paper parallel to the first line. This is your top hip line.

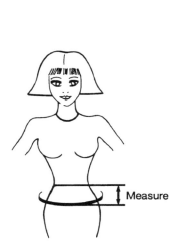

Diagram 4

Measure around your top hip, and mark a quarter of this measurement on the line in your diagram. On my diagram it is 23 cm (9").

Diagram 5

Now from your waist, measure down to the thickest part of your body (on my diagram it is 24 cm (9½") down from the waist line). Draw a line parallel to your waist and top hip lines. This line is called the hip line.

Measure

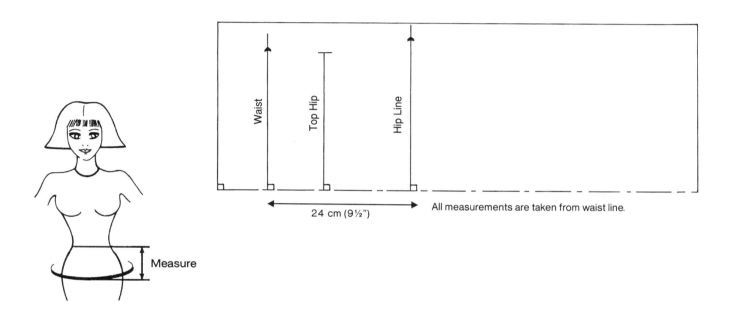

Waist

Top Hip

Hip Line

24 cm (9½")

All measurements are taken from waist line.

Diagram 6

Measure your full hip, and mark a quarter of the distance on the hip line. On my diagram it is 24 cm (9½").

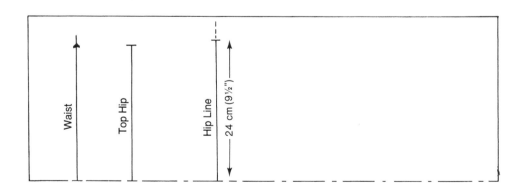

Waist

Top Hip

Hip Line

24 cm (9½")

Measure

Diagram 7

Place the flexible ruler on the hip line. As it touches the top hip line, the ruler will naturally curve towards the waist line.

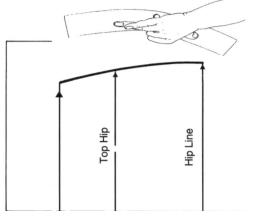

By holding the ruler in between your index and middle finger, and exerting pressure with your ring finger and thumb from the other side of the ruler, you will get a slight curve suitable for hip line.

Top Hip

Hip Line

Diagram 8

Draw a line from the hip line parallel to the centre fold down to the required skirt length; connect the two lines at the required skirt length with a right-angled line from the centre fold. This is the first step in creating a paper pattern for your skirt.

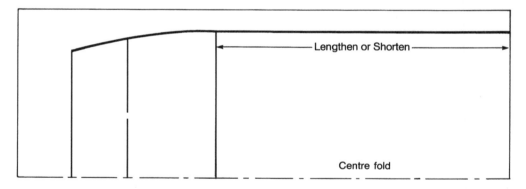

Lengthen or Shorten

Centre fold

Diagram 9

Cut out the paper pattern for the skirt, then cut the skirt out in calico. Fold a skirt length in the calico, then halve the fabric again, leaving the selvage edge 2 cm (¾") wider (this will form the centre back and a fold at the centre front). *Do not forget the 2 cm (¾")seam allowance.* (Sew side seams only, no darts at this stage.) Sew up side and back seam, leaving room to try the skirt on. You need to make sure skirt fits on the hipline before you continue. This works best in 150 cm (60") calico.

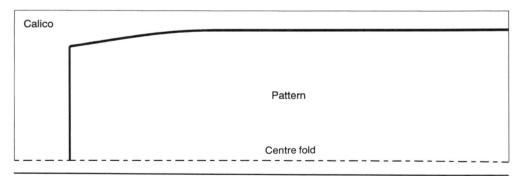

Calico

Pattern

Centre fold

Addition for Centre Back Seam

Diagram 10

On fitting the skirt around the waist, the darts will form naturally. Pin the darts in. Standing sideways to a mirror, the front or back waist can be lifted to get the side seam straight. Now mark in the darts and waist. Transfer the front and back darts to the paper pattern, creating a front and back skirt pattern.

Make sure side seam is straight

Diagram 11

With a different coloured pen straighten the lines using your ruler. For pattern making you need to use the corrected straight lines, rather than the personal fitted ones. However, when you actually stitch the darts you should follow the original lines for a proper fit.

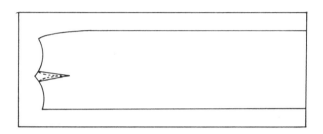

Diagram 12

Fold the darts using the corner of a table (see Diagram 5 on page 42). While the dart is folded, rule a curved line connecting the waist front and back. Cut along this line while the dart remains folded. You have now obtained the correct waist line.

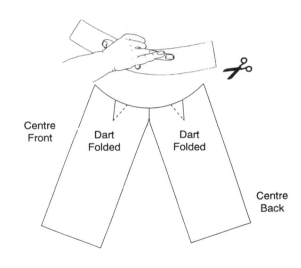

Centre Front

Dart Folded

Dart Folded

Centre Back

Diagram 13

On opening the paper, the darts should have an inverted V shape at the edge of the paper. You now have your straight basic skirt pattern.

Once you have made up the basic skirt I suggest you make the gored skirt, flared skirt and skirt with yoke, all shown on page 61, following the instructions in chapters 9, 10 and 11. This will give you more confidence when you come to constructing the bodice in the next chapter.

Point

CHAPTER 2
Creating the Bodice

PAPER

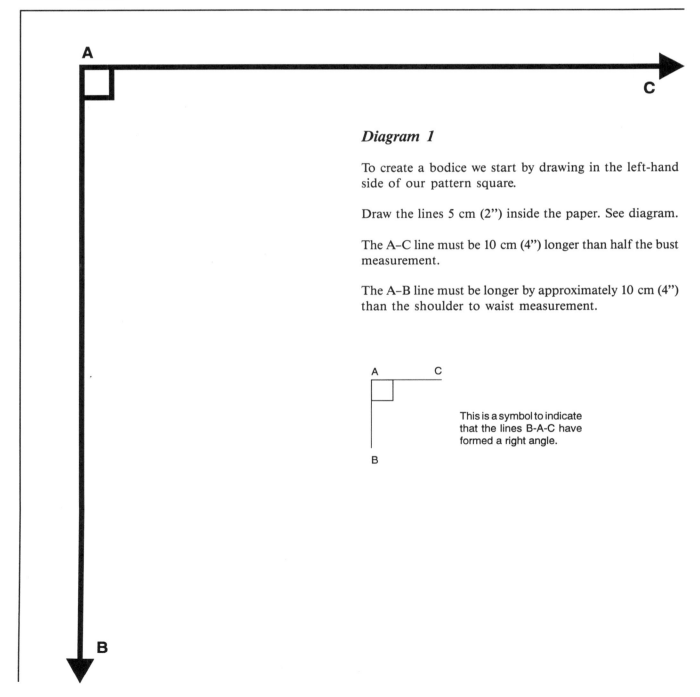

Diagram 1

To create a bodice we start by drawing in the left-hand side of our pattern square.

Draw the lines 5 cm (2") inside the paper. See diagram.

The A–C line must be 10 cm (4") longer than half the bust measurement.

The A–B line must be longer by approximately 10 cm (4") than the shoulder to waist measurement.

This is a symbol to indicate that the lines B-A-C have formed a right angle.

Dolman Sleeves and Basic Skirt
The dolman top is made from a cotton knit jersey.
The basic skirt is spotted cotton. The waist is
elasticised.
Dolman sleeves, page 67; basic skirt, page 11.

Skirt with Yoke
Fully lined skirt with yoke, made in pink linen.
Construction see page 66.

A

½ Bust measurement

D C

B

Diagram 2

Measure your bust. Be careful to take the tape measure across your bust loosely, take care that the tape measure does not drop around your back, and make sure you are measuring the wide part of your back. Do not breathe in or out when getting this measurement.

On taking this measurement add 5 cm (2"). Fold the tape in half and mark this measurement on the A–C line. Call the mark D.

Write down your own measurements for half bust measurements:

Half Bust = _____ cm

_____ inches

Front   Back

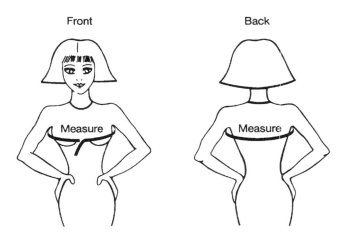

Measure   Measure

Diagram 3

Now draw from D down E. This line will be parallel to A–B. (See next step for length of lines.)

Mark the corners as centre front (CF) and centre back (CB).

Diagram 4 (see next page)

Measure shoulder to waist-front and shoulder to waist-back to form the bottom of the rectangle. Do this by putting your hands on your waist (you automatically get your waist), then run the tape measure from the waist-point on the front, up across your bust, over your shoulder

and down to the waist-back as in Diagram 4. Then check, or get someone to check, the measurement at the shoulder-point.

Your index finger and your thumb indicate the waistline as in the picture. A simple way is to start the tape measure at the front index finger taking it across your shoulder to your thumb at the back. Hold onto the back waist measurement (the front is the end of the tape).

Using your other hand, simply pinch the tape at the shoulder line and lift it off the body. This will automatically give you your front and back waist measurements. Transfer to your paper. Mark from the A–D line down to F and F for the back and G and G for the front, joining the points F and F together and the points G and G.

As an example, the overall measurement might be 84 cm (33"); if the front shoulder to waist is 44 cm (17¼"), the back is 40 cm (15¾") long. Mark the back measurement, 40 cm (15¾"), at F on both the lines DE and AB; mark the front measurement, 44 cm (17¼") at G on both lines. Draw in the two parallel lines to indicate the back waist position and the front waist position.

In some instances, there are variations on these lines, i.e. they could be the same for someone with a very small bust; for a fuller figure the distance for the front would be longer than on the diagram; and yet again, with a forward stance, the back measurement could be longer.

For now, mark these measurements in. When we have finished the full block, and if your back is longer, see the alterations before cutting it out in calico. See The Longer Back in Chapter 6.

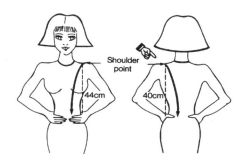

Measurements are found by putting hands on waist in this position.

A   D   C

CF   CB

F   Back waist = _____ cm (_____ inches)   F

G   Front waist = _____ cm (_____ inches)   G   E

B

Diagram 5

Place your thumb under your armpit. Rest your hand on your chest. Measure from shoulder to index finger as indicated on drawing to find your shoulder to chest measurement.

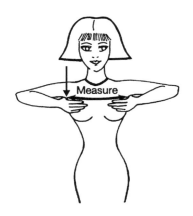

Measure down from the A–D line and draw in line XY parallel to the A–D line. On an average body this measurement can be anything from 15 cm (5¾") to 20 cm (8").

Shoulder to Chest Measurement:

_____ cm

_____ inches

A _____ D

CF   CB

Approx. 15 cm to 20 cm (5¾" to 8")

X _____ Y

B

22

Diagram 6

When you put your arms down, there is a crease on your body at the point where your thumb was. Measure across the front from crease to crease, fold tape in half and mark in the half front chest measurement on the X–Y line.

Half Front Chest Measurement:

_____ cm

_____ inches

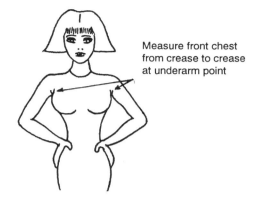

Measure front chest from crease to crease at underarm point

A   D

CF   CB

X   Half Front Chest 18 cm (7¼")   Y

B

Diagram 7

Similarly, there is a crease on your back when your arm is down. Measure from crease to crease across the back, fold tape in half, mark in from the right end of the X–Y line.

On my diagram it is 19 cm (7½").

Half Back Chest Measurement:

_____ cm

_____ inches

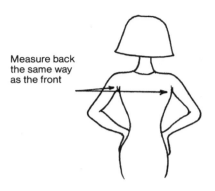

Measure back
the same way
as the front

A **D**

CF **CB**

X Half Front Chest Measurement | Chest line | Half Back Chest 19 cm (7½") **Y**

B

Diagram 8

Find the width of your shoulder by measuring from the left shoulder point to the right shoulder point, across your back. Halve that measurement and mark it in from the centre back towards the middle of your diagram. On my diagram this is 20 cm (8").

Back Shoulder to Shoulder Measurement

_____ cm

_____ inches

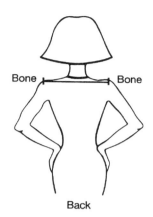

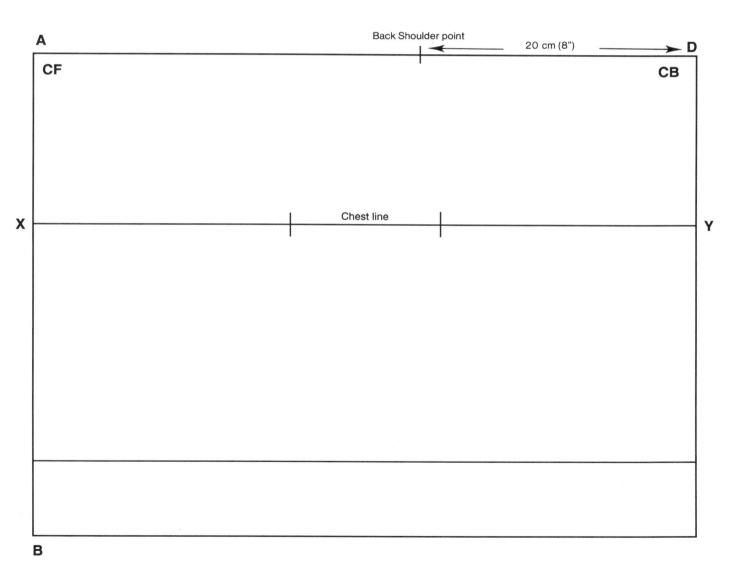

Diagram 9

Measure the same points on the front to find the front shoulder. This measuring may be a bit uncomfortable, but do not forget that we have not yet cut out the neckline. On my diagram this measurement is 19 cm (7½"). Mark it in on your diagram.

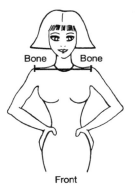

Half Front Shoulder to Shoulder Measurement:

_____ cm

_____ inches

19 cm (7½")   Front shoulder point

CF   CB

Shirt with Six-gored Skirt
The shirt, in white cotton, is made from the same pattern as the shirt dress on the next page, but cut shorter. It is worn with a six-gored white linen skirt with gathers at the waist.
(Shirt, page 73; six-gored skirt, page 62.)

Shirt Dress
Made in polished cotton with set-in sleeves.
Construction see page 73.

Diagram 10

Most neck measurements are approximately 15 cm (5¾")
across, therefore we take half this, i.e. 7.5 cm (3"), and
we mark this in on both the centre front and centre back,
in towards the middle of the diagram. (This measurement
has to be identical for the front and the back so that your
finished pattern will balance.) Note that the front shoulder
measurement is smaller than the back shoulder measurement, however, allowing for the back dart to be fitted in
calico at a later stage.

Note:
An adult male could be 8 cm (3½") or a child 5 cm (2").

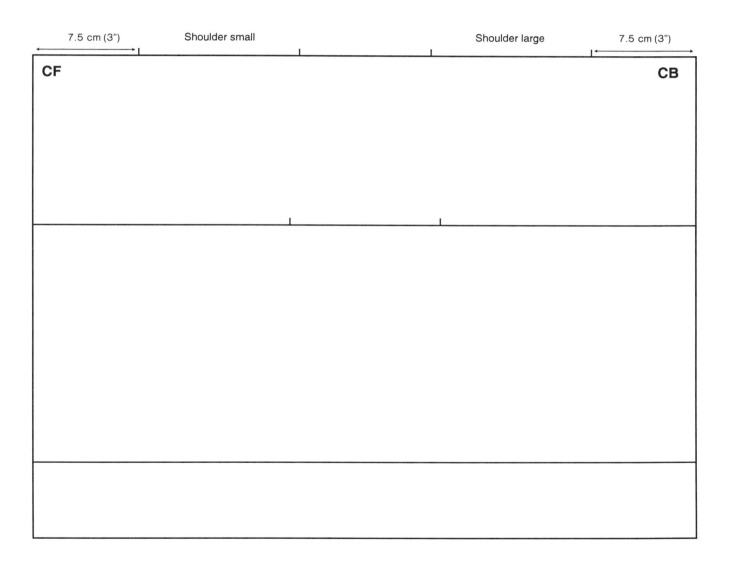

Diagram 11

Our shoulders are not horizontal but angle down slightly. I have found from experience an approximate angle that fits onto most bodies. This is done by marking a point 1 cm (⅜") above the front and back neck points, and another 1 cm (⅜") below the front and back shoulder points. Join these points as shown on the diagram.

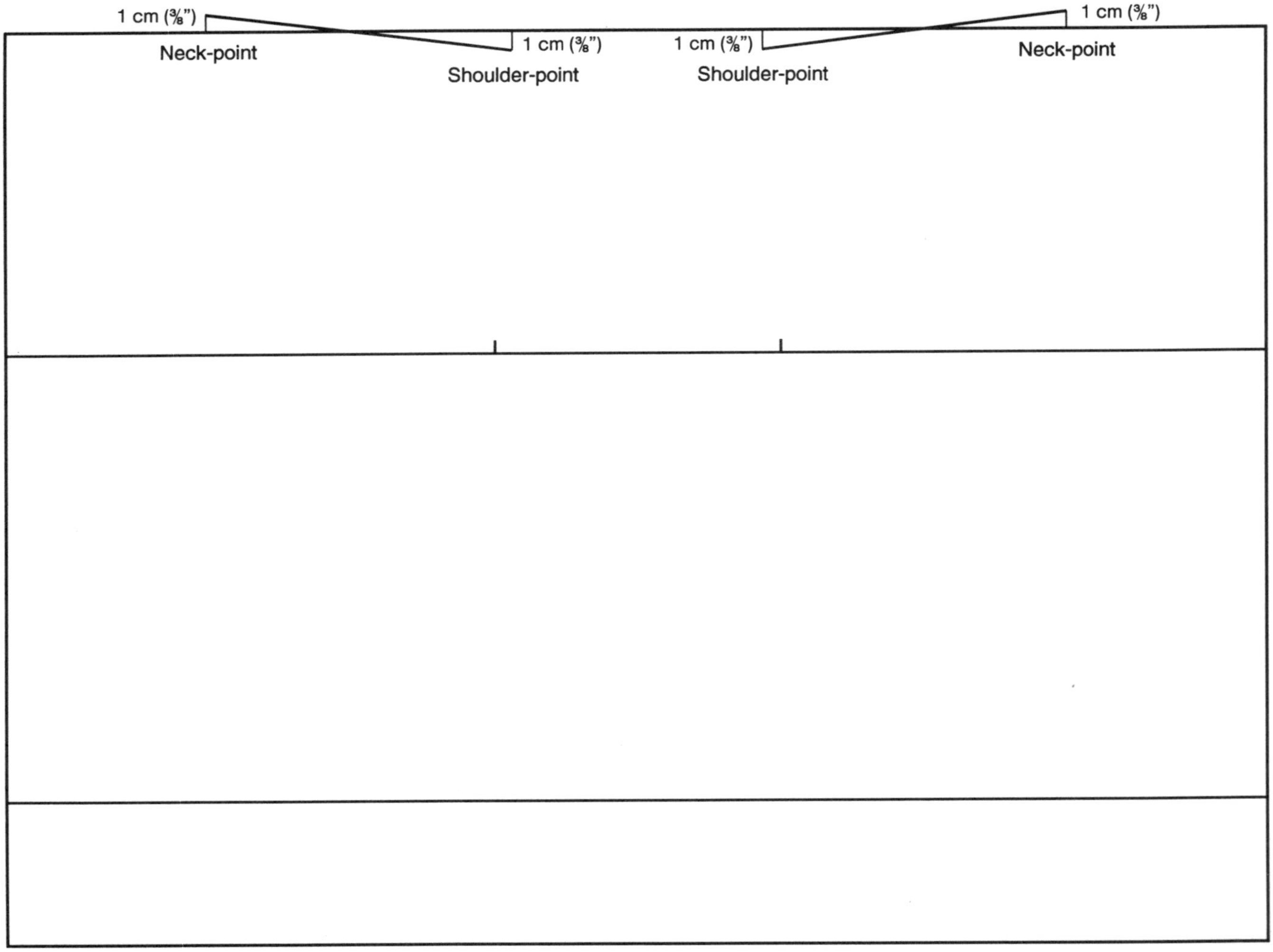

1 cm (⅜")   1 cm (⅜")

Neck-point   1 cm (⅜")   1 cm (⅜")   Neck-point

Shoulder-point   Shoulder-point

Diagram 12

To draw in the neckline, measure 7 cm (2¾") down from the centre front along the line A–B. The simplest way to connect the neck-point to the shoulder-point is to use your flexible ruler on its edge. This should form the perfect curve.

The ruler will fully curve held by index and thumb on one end and the remaining three fingers on the other end as shown here.

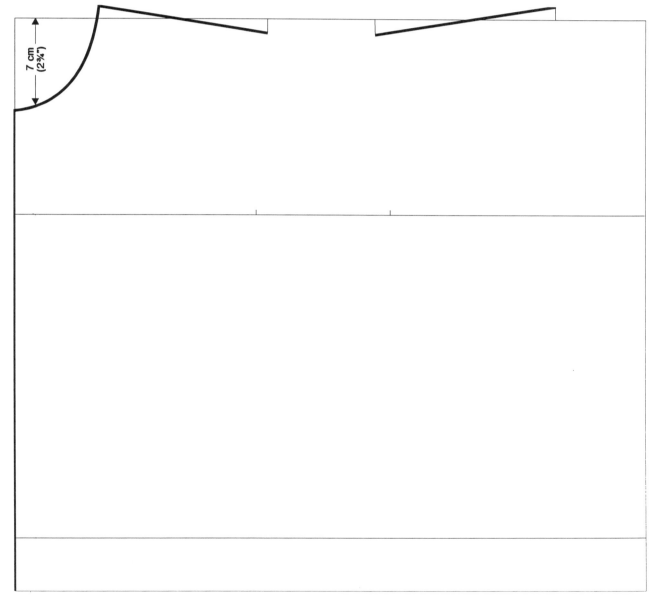

Diagram 13

To draw in the centre back neckline, set the flexible ruler on its edge and join the centre back of the diagram to the raised shoulder-point.

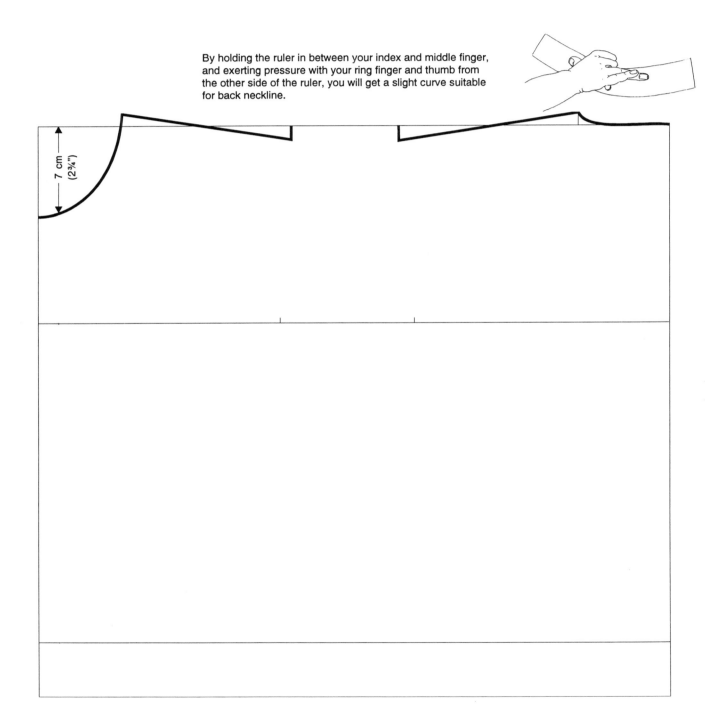

By holding the ruler in between your index and middle finger, and exerting pressure with your ring finger and thumb from the other side of the ruler, you will get a slight curve suitable for back neckline.

7 cm (2¾")

Diagram 14

Now divide your diagram to separate your front and back. Do this by finding the centre of your diagram and adding 1 cm (⅜") to the measurement for the front. Draw a line from the top to the bottom of the diagram. On my diagram this line is 24 cm (9½") in from the centre front line.

If your armhole space is very narrow (approx. 5 or 6 cm or 2 to 2½") draw the line at the centre. The other exception to this rule is when the back is wider than the front, when the back should be 1 cm (⅜") wider.

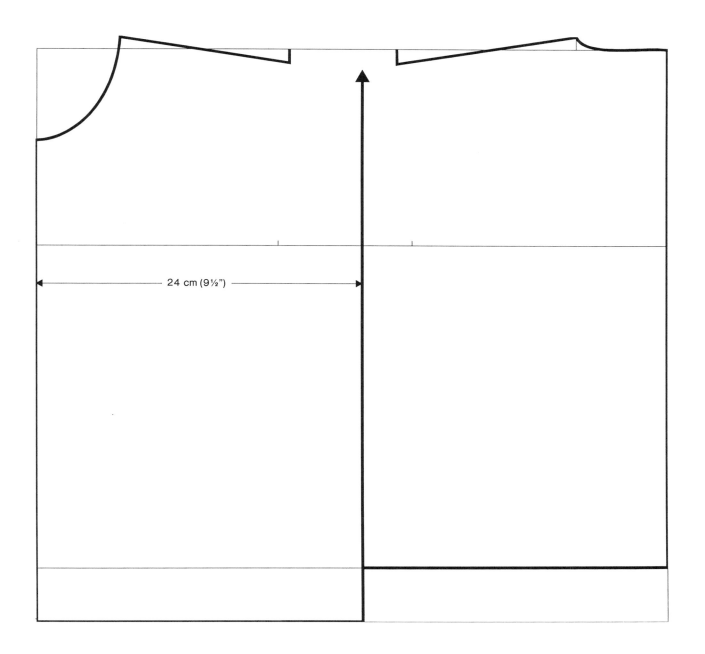

24 cm (9½")

Diagram 15

Find your armhole measurement. Do this by measuring the distance from your waist to the position under your arm where you would like your armhole to finish (some people like their armhole very high, some very low).

Mark this measurement from the higher waist line. On my diagram this is the back waist line. The exception is when the back is longer. On my diagram I have made the underarm measurement line 19 cm (7½") long.

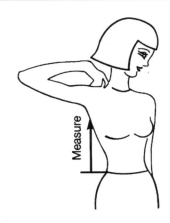

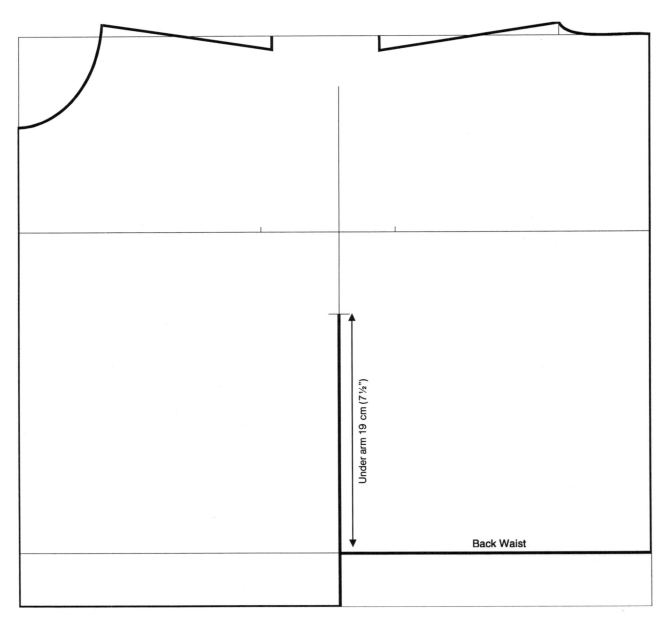

Under arm 19 cm (7½")

Back Waist

Diagram 16

Make the armhole shape by joining up 5 points — the front shoulder-point, front chest-point, underarm-point, back chest-point, and back shoulder-point. This can be done by setting the flexible ruler on edge again to form the correct U shape (see diagram).

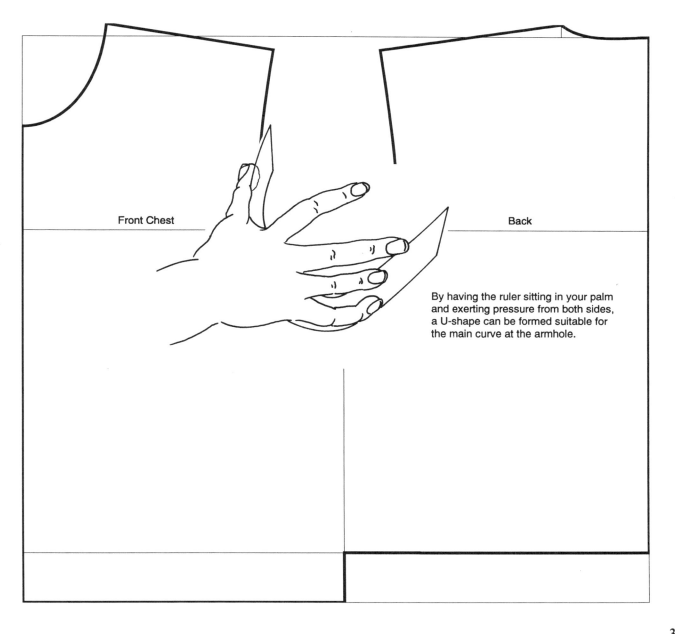

Front Chest

Back

By having the ruler sitting in your palm and exerting pressure from both sides, a U-shape can be formed suitable for the main curve at the armhole.

Diagram 17

Congratulations! Now you have your basic front and back shapes. Now we are going to work on the most important part of your basic pattern design. This is to find your bust-point, in pattern-making called a pivot-point. When you become experienced in your pattern-making, knowing this point will enable you to re-design and re-shape all your patterns.

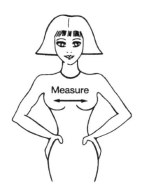

Now I will explain how to create this important point. Firstly, you measure from one bust-point to the other and halve that measurement, which on my diagram is 10 cm (4"). Draw this from the centre front inwards towards the centre of your front pattern (see diagram).

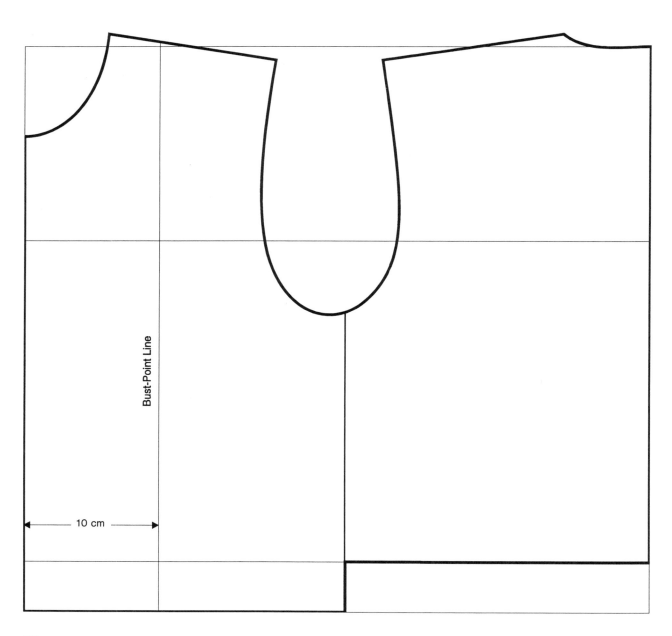

Bust-Point Line

◄— 10 cm —►

Diagram 18

From the centre of your shoulder measure down to your bust-point. Mark the bust-point line with a cross. In this diagram it is 26 cm (10¼") down.

Note that the shaping at waist and at darts will form automatically. See next chapter.

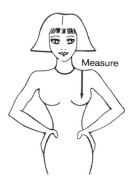

Measure

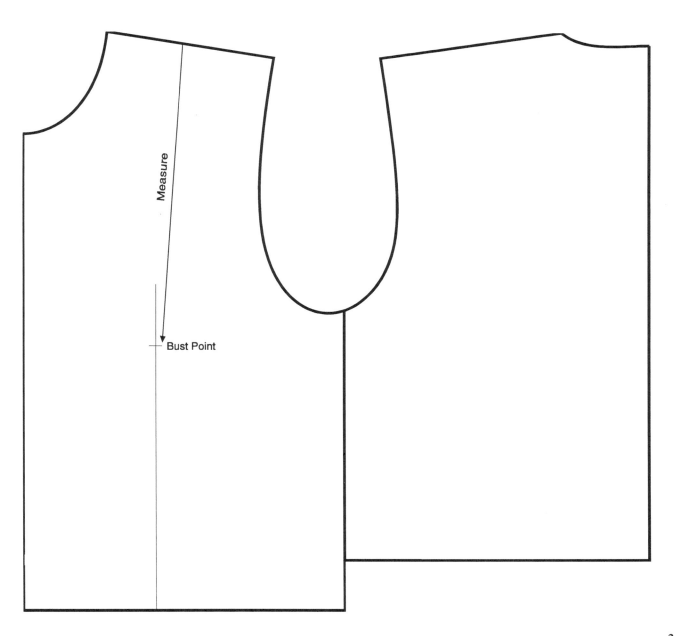

Measure

Bust Point

CHAPTER 3
Fitting the Calico

This section deals with cutting the paper pattern into calico and then fitting it.

A special note to those with a longer back: Before continuing, alter your pattern following the instructions in Chapter 6 (page 51).

Diagram 1

Cut out the front pattern piece, making sure you follow the front waist-line. Follow the back waist line for the back pattern piece.

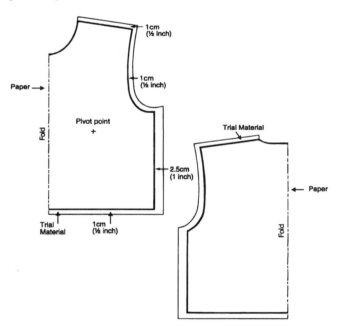

Lay the pattern pieces on the folded calico, placing the centre front and centre back on the fold. Cut out the calico, adding seam allowances as shown in the diagram. On pinning and fitting the calico, you will find the surplus length between your front and back side seams will fold, creating the foldline for your bust dart naturally. Other darts will form the same way.

The following instructions and diagrams will give the perfect fit.

Diagram 2

The first two pins are to hold the front and back together at neck point.

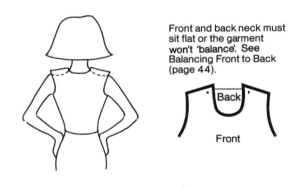

Front and back neck must sit flat or the garment won't 'balance'. See Balancing Front to Back (page 44).

Diagram 3

The next two pins are at the shoulder points, following the slope of the shoulder and showing if a dart is needed.

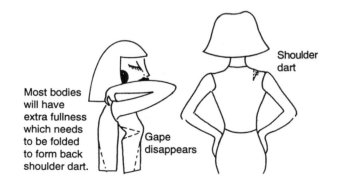

Most bodies will have extra fullness which needs to be folded to form back shoulder dart.

Gape disappears

Shoulder dart

Diagram 4

Pin the shoulder dart if needed.

Diagram 5

Pin once under each arm.

Diagram 6

Two pins at waist, fitting in the waist.

Diagram 7

Pin bust dart, which will form if needed.

Diagram 8

Remove the pin from the waist. Adjust and pin the side seams.

Diagram 9

Pin the front and back waist darts.

Diagram 10

Do any other necessary adjustments.

Diagram 11

Draw in the positions of the darts with a marker pen on the better fitting side.

Diagram 12

Finally, if the garment is to open at centre front, cut up the centre front of the calico bodice, which will open on an angle.

Add the amount missing on your pattern and mark it as a new centre front grain for all your front opening garments. This will prevent your front opening garments pulling open.

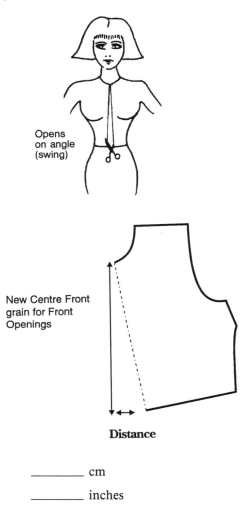

Opens on angle (swing)

New Centre Front grain for Front Openings

Distance

_____ cm

_____ inches

Write your measurements here so that you can create your own front opening garments.

CHAPTER 4
Creating the Basic Pattern from Calico

Diagram 1

Set original front and back paper patterns on top of the cut out calico with any extra darts drawn, placing the paper in exactly the same position. Refer back to Diagram 1 on page 38. The markings on the calico might look like this.

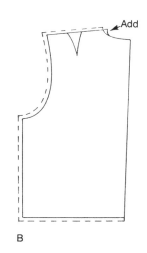

A

B

Diagram 2

Transfer your personal fittings and adjustments from the calico to the paper pattern.

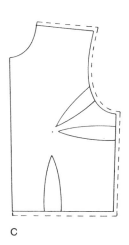

C

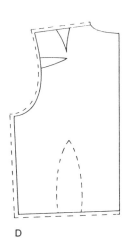

D

Diagram 3

With a different coloured pen straighten the darts using a ruler. For pattern-making you need to use the corrected curved lines (see dotted lines in drawing) rather than the personal straight ones. However, when you sew the pattern you should go back to the original lines.

Note: The bust dart and the front and back darts formed from the waist form an outward curve, while the shoulder dart forms an inward curve. Follow the instructions and the garment will mould to your body shape.

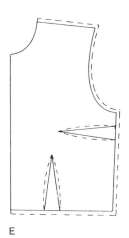

E

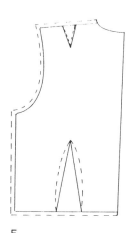

F

Diagram 4

Glue some extra paper to the top of the back shoulder pattern.

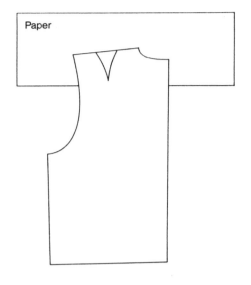

Diagram 6

While the dart is folded, rule a straight line connecting the shoulder point to the neck point. Extend this line and mark in any addition, filling in the neck if needed.

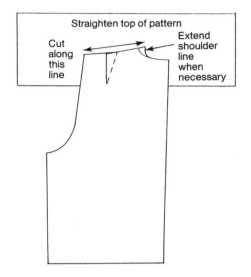

Diagram 5

Working on a sharp-edged table with right-angled corners, place the point of the dart to the corner of the table. Follow the sharp table edge to create a crease on the paper. Place your index finger at the point of the dart, right at the corner of the table. With your other hand fold the creased line on top of the uncreased line. The dart is now folded.

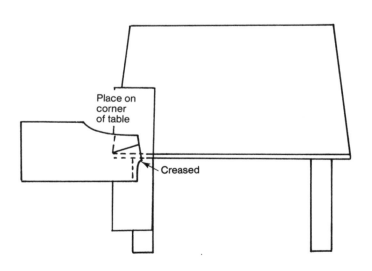

Diagram 7

Cut along this line while the dart is folded. You have now obtained the correct shoulder line. The shoulder dart should have an inverted V shape when it is opened out.

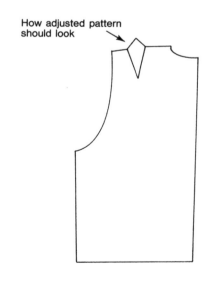

Diagram 8

Correct and reshape the back armhole. If there is a dart in the back armhole, pivot it (see Chapter 5, The Pivot Point) to either the waist or the shoulder dart, depending which way it points. (This will only occur with a body which has hunched or rolled shoulders.)

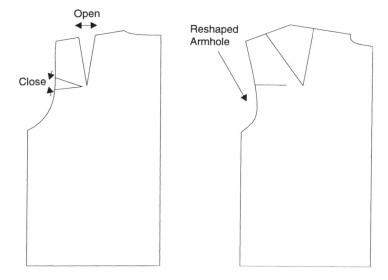

Diagram 9

Straighten the side seam. Fold back the waist dart but *do not cut.*

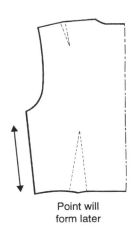

Balancing Front to Back

Diagram 10

Begin checking the front pattern at the neck. Add paper at the front neck/shoulder line as you did for the back neck point (page 42) and rule in the shoulder line.

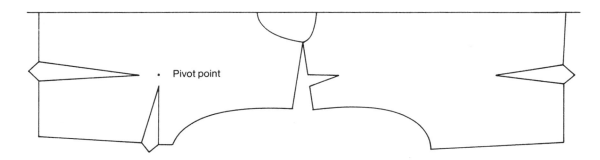

Place the centre back pattern against a straight line, e.g. a ruler or table edge. Place the centre front pattern against the same straight line, neck and shoulder lines opposite each other. Move the back neck shoulder point until it touches the front shoulder line. This is your front neck/shoulder point. Fix the front neck from this point. Now your pattern is balanced.

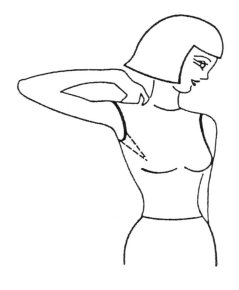

Diagram 11

Correct and reshape the front armhole. If there is a dart in the front armhole, pivot it (see Chapter 5, The Pivot Point) to either the waist or the bust dart depending which way it points. There should be an even amount of fullness in the bust and the waist darts. There could be more than one pivot point until the basic block is completed.

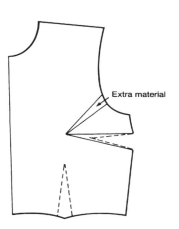

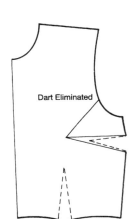

Shirt with Rolled Collar
The shirt is made from printed red satin.
Construction see page 71.

Vest and Flared Skirt
Basic shirt with Chinese neckline and flared skirt made from printed polyester. The vest is made from yellow denim. Shirt page 73; Chinese neckline pages 61, 71; and vest (page 70)

Diagram 12

The armhole must form a smooth line or the sleeves will pull later on.

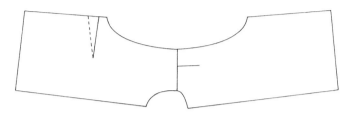

Diagram 13

Working down the front side, fold the bust dart using the corner of a table (the dart must face towards the waist).

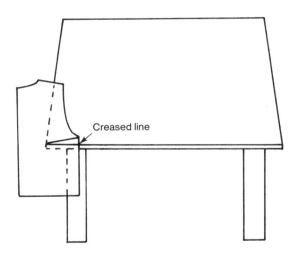

Diagram 14

Now cut along the front side seam line, making sure the side seams are the same length as the back.

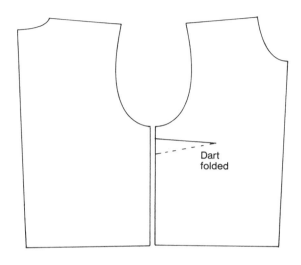

Diagram 15

Fold the front waist dart but *do not cut*.

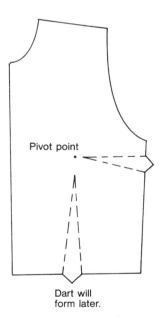

Diagram 16

Put the front and back sides together. Curve a line from centre front waist line to side seams. Continue to centre back waist line to get your waist. This could be a curved shape as in the diagram. An S shape can form with a large midriff or longer back.

Diagram 17

This is your own individual block basic pattern. When all darts are marked in, the block should look like the diagram below.

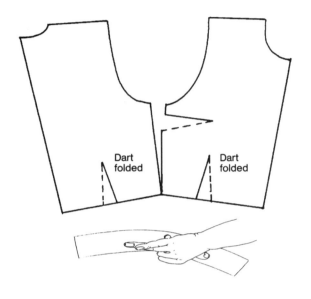

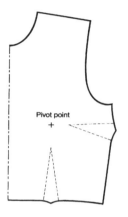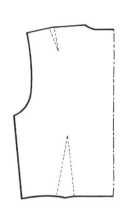

* The dart shapes are formed during fitting as you cut across material or paper while darts are folded.

Diagram 18

Cut the basic pattern in calico with a zip at the back. Check the fit of the bodice. It should follow the body contours firmly, but not tightly. It should be made firmer for a strapless top, but add at least 5 cm (2") more at the side seams, evenly at front and back, for a day dress.

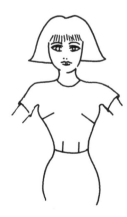

CHAPTER 5
The Pivot Point

Once you have the pivot point as explained below, you can draw a line from that point to any of the points marked A, B, C, D in this diagram. When you close the original bust dart, the line you have cut through will automatically open, as shown in the series of diagrams 5A to 5D.

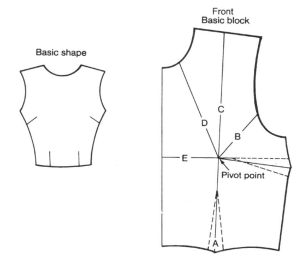

Basic shape

Front
Basic block

Pivoting Darts

Find the centre of a dart. Rule a line across from the centre to the dart point, dividing the dart in half, e.g. ⋀. Continue this line for some distance. Repeat this with the other dart you intend to pivot. Where the two lines meet is the pivot point. Cut along both lines to the point, without cutting the point. Now you can add or eliminate one of the darts (the fullness will transfer to the other dart).

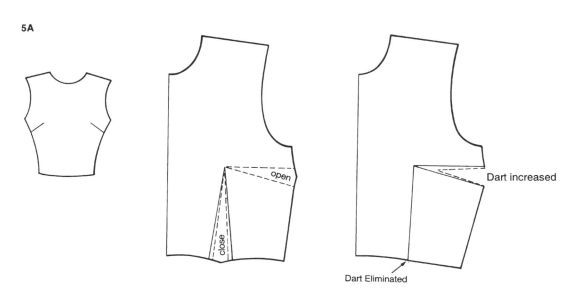

5A

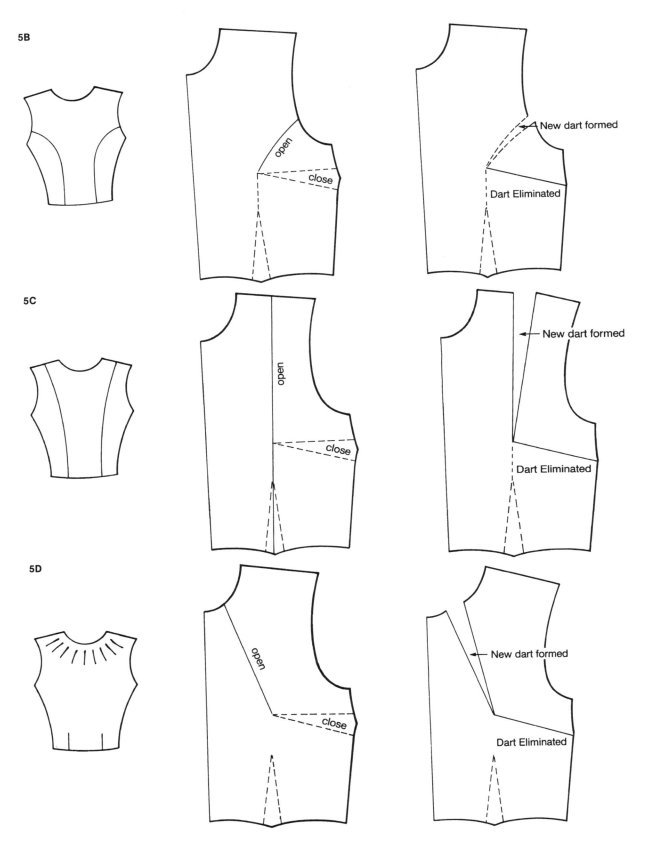

5B

5C

5D

open
close
New dart formed
Dart Eliminated

open
close
New dart formed
Dart Eliminated

open
close
New dart formed
Dart Eliminated

Almost any design can be achieved by using the above diagrams. You can, of course, either dart the new openings or gather the fabric at these points, depending on the style of the garment.

CHAPTER 6
Problem Solving

For the Longer Back

When the back measurement is longer than the front (refer page 48) before you cut the calico on page 41 you will need to follow these instructions.

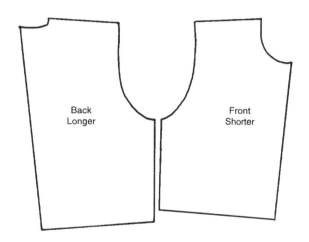

Form a dart approximately midway down the side seam on the back bodice. The dart must measure the same distance as the extra length between the front and back bodice.

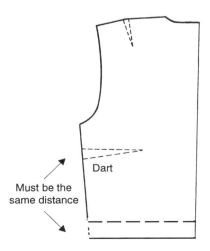

Transfer this dart to the middle of the back shoulder. See picture below.

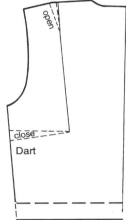

By opening the dart at the shoulder and closing the dart at the side seam you will achieve the following: There will be a dart to accommodate the curvature at the shoulder, and the centre back will remain longer where this particular body shape will need the extra length. See drawing below.

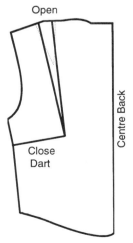

Now cut your altered back pattern in calico as on page 41, then follow the instructions for fitting the calico as on page 38.

For the Large Midriff

This will be handled mainly in the fitting of your calico.

For women whose front measurement is more than 7 cm (2½") longer than their back, some of this measurement will form the bust dart (see page 38, Diagram 6); shape the remainder from the centre front back to the waistline (see example below). Note: When a man has the front bodice pattern longer than the back measurement in the fitting of the calico, you may find that his waist is shaped similar to the shape in this diagram without the bust dart.

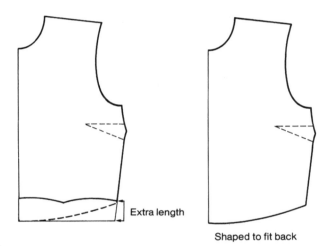

Extra length

Shaped to fit back

CHAPTER 7
The Sleeves

Diagram 1

Using the basic block paper pattern, pin the front shoulder and the back shoulder together, and pin under the arm, to see the armhole form. Using a tape measure, measure from the outer shoulder down towards the armhole, as shown by the arrow in the diagram. This is your sleeve height measurement. The average sleeve height is about 16.5 cm (6½").

Sleeve height

_____ cm

_____ inches

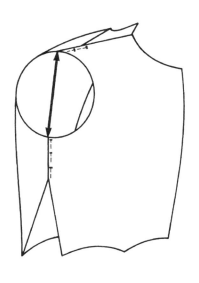

Diagram 2

To draw a sleeve pattern, start by drawing a straight line, the measurement of the sleeve height. On my diagram it is 16.5 cm (6½").

Sleeve height point

Diagram 3

Measure the circumference of your arm at the thickest part of your upper arm and add 4 to 5 cm (1½"–2"). On my diagram it is 34 cm (13¾") along the line CD. Now draw a line at a right angle to the sleeve height, making it half your arm measurement. On my diagram it is 17 cm (6¾"). Mark points A and B as per diagram.

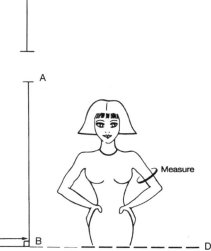

A

C — Half the arm measurement — B

Measure

D

Full arm measurement

The underarm part of the sleeve is the same shape as the underarm of the block. Use the front and back block to create this shape for the sleeve, following Diagrams 4 and 5.

Diagram 4

Turn the back bodice block over, place the armhole point to point D on the sleeve pattern and follow the line of the armhole up for about 2.5 cm (1") with your marker.

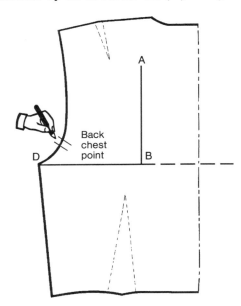

Diagram 5

Turn front bodice block over, place armhole point to point C on the sleeve pattern. Follow the line of the armhole up for about 2.5 cm (1") as in the diagram.

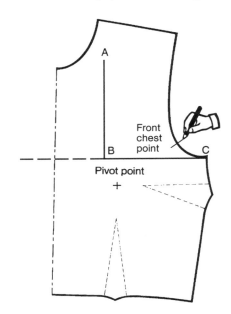

Diagram 6

Placing your flexible ruler, a tape measure or an electrical cord on the points C, A and D will allow the bell shape of the sleeve to form.

The rule is—it must touch points A, C and D and make a bell shape.

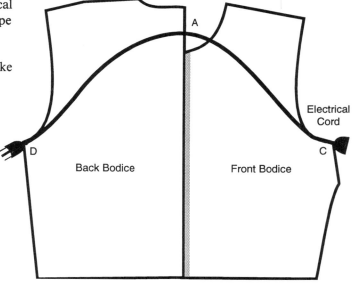

Diagram 7

Measure the front and back armholes and mark the resulting figures on the front and back sleeve. The space between the measurements is the easing.

The rule is—*Metric*: For every 2.5 cm you need approximately 3 mm of easing. *Imperial*: For every 1" you need ⅛" easing.

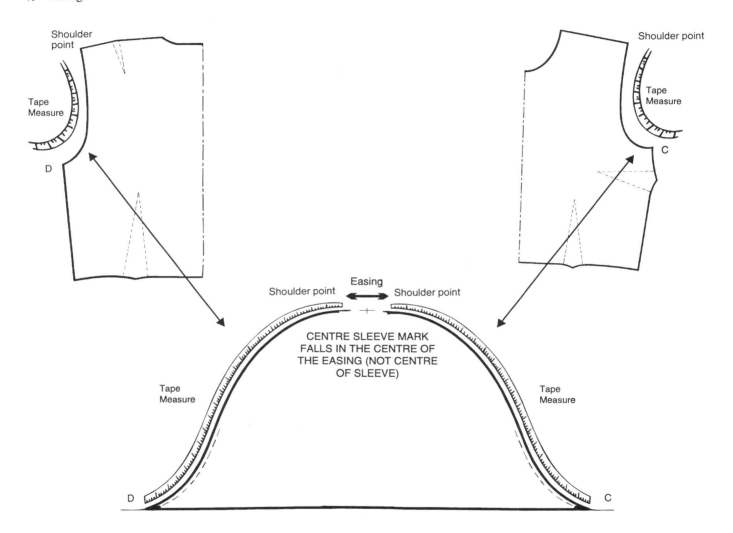

Diagram 8

Cut out and try the sleeve pattern against the arm to check the fitting.

Diagram 9

The sleeve can be made smaller or larger by adjusting the original pattern, keeping the rule in mind.

The rule is—*Metric*: For every 2.5 cm you need approximately 3 mm of easing. *Imperial*: For every 1" you need ⅛" easing.

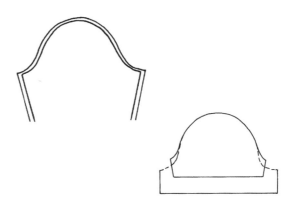

Diagram 10

The length and width of the sleeve changes according to the style desired. When you achieve the proper head shape for the sleeve, and it will fit into the bodice, you are on the right track.

When the sleeve head is completed, it may be slightly larger than the armhole, and the surplus can be eased for a perfect fit.

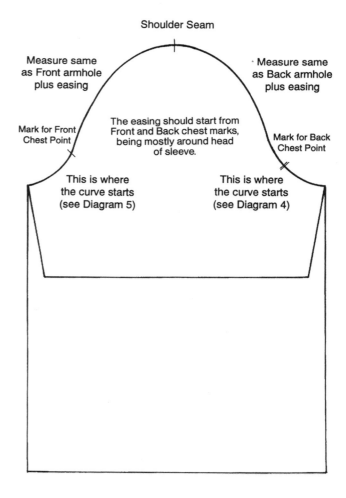

Shoulder Seam

Measure same as Front armhole plus easing

Measure same as Back armhole plus easing

Mark for Front Chest Point

The easing should start from Front and Back chest marks, being mostly around head of sleeve.

Mark for Back Chest Point

This is where the curve starts (see Diagram 5)

This is where the curve starts (see Diagram 4)

CHAPTER 8
Creating Collars

Shirt Collar

Diagram 1

Measure half your neck line.

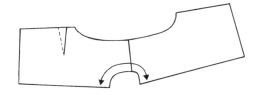

Diagram 2

Draw a straight line measuring half the neck line. Mark in front, back and shoulder point.

Diagram 3
Draw a line parallel to original line and 5 cm (2") above it.

Diagram 4

Connect ends to form a rectangle. Name sides centre front and centre back.

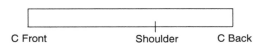

Diagram 5

At centre front create a point by extending top line by 2.5 cm (1"), then connect it to the centre front point.

Diagram 6

Cut the collar out in paper then calico, with centre back on fold. Try it on. The collar should be sitting high at the back and around the shoulders.

Peter Pan Collar

Diagram 1

Draw Peter Pan collar on your calico bodice.

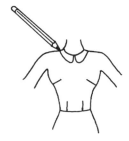

Diagram 2

Draw the upper part of the front bodice on the paper; draw the upper part of the back bodice, connecting the shoulders.

Transfer the front collar design from the calico to your paper, continuing the line to the back.

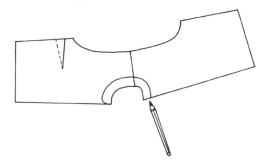

Diagram 3

Cut the collar out in paper, then calico. Try it on. The collar should sit flat around your neck.

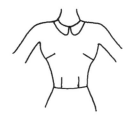

Chinese Collar

Diagram 1

Measure half your neckline on a line. Mark the front, back and shoulder.

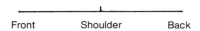

Diagram 2

Draw a line 2.5 cm (1") above and parallel to the first line.

Diagram 3

Connect sides to form a rectangle. Mark in front, back and shoulder seam.

Diagram 4

Drop front 2 cm (¾"). Lift back 1 cm (⅜").

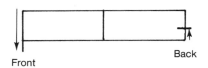

Diagram 5

Draw in curved line to connect these points.

Diagram 6

Draw a line 2.5 cm (1") above and parallel to original curved line.

Diagram 7

Curve front end of collar.

Diagram 8

Collar will stand evenly around the neck.

Rolled Collar

Diagram 1

Measure your full neck line.

Draw a rectangle approximately 10 cm (4") wide and the length of your neck measurement. This is the collar pattern.

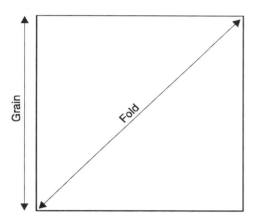

Find the bias on a square of calico and fold along it.

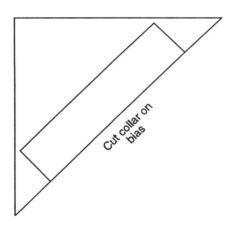

Place the collar pattern on the bias and cut it out. Try it on.

Other Types of Collars

When you examine the construction of the Peter Pan collar and the shirt collar you will realise that the straighter the neckline on a collar, the higher the collar will sit; the more curved the neckline, the lower the collar will sit. Now try this technique.

Collar Design

Diagram 1

Draw a collar on your calico bodice.

Diagram 2

Draw your front bodice on paper. Transfer the front collar design to your paper.

(Turn to next page.)

Diagram 3

Decide if you want the collar to sit flat on your garment or be raised at the neckline.

Add approximately 1 cm (⅜") to the neckline if you want the collar to get that rolled look, and widen the neckline by the same amount.

Diagram 4

Curve the line from this point, extending the line to a distance equal to half your neck measurement. Do this for top and bottom of the collar. Square the back neckpoint.

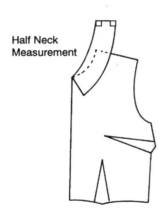

Diagram 5

Cut out the collar in paper first, then calico. Try it on. The collar should sit around the neck as you originally decided. If the result is what you want, adjust your bodice pattern to match.

Chapters 9 to 17 give instructions for the garments below. Drafting these patterns will improve your pattern-making skills.

Shirt dress (page 73)

Evening top (page 74)

Skirt with yoke (page 66)

Shirt with Chinese collar (pages 61, 71)

Vest (page 70)

Flared skirt

Sleeveless top (page 68)

Gored skirt (page 62)

Top with dolman sleeves (page 67)

Basic skirt (page 11)

Shirt with rolled collar (page 71)

CHAPTER 9

Gored Skirt

A gored skirt is made up of waist to hem sections, each referred to as a gore. A picture of this garment appears on the facing page.

1. Use a fresh pattern paper and draw in the skirt block with the centre front on the fold.
2. Divide your full waist, top hip and hip measurements by the number of gores you want × 2.
   Example: 4 gore skirt—the waist, top hip, hip is ÷ 8
   6 gore skirt—the waist, top hip, hip is ÷ 12
   8 gore skirt—the waist, top hip, hip is ÷ 16
4. Mark the new waist, top hip and hip on the lines on your pattern. The measurements will be very small. Connect the points using the flexible ruler as shown in Diagrams 7–8 on page 14.

Diagram 2

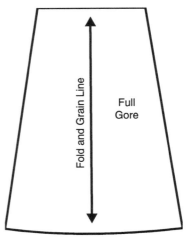

5. Drop a vertical line from the hip to the hemline, and add 10 cm (4") flare at the hemline.
6. Connect the hem to your hip line. (The lines must be equal in length.) See Diagram 1.
7. Cut out your new pattern and open it up. You will have a full gore. See Diagram 2. The number of gores you need will depend on which skirt you started with, e.g. 4 gores for a 4-gore skirt.
8. Add appropriate seams, skirt band or facing. Now it is ready to sew.

Diagram 1

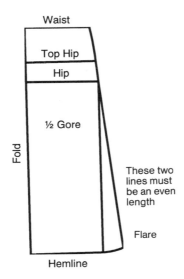

Sleeveless Top and Gored Skirt
The sleeveless top is made in black crepe, fully lined with red printed satin, the same material as the shirt. The 6-gored skirt is made from lightweight polyester elasticised at the waist.
(Sleeveless top, page 68.)
(Gored skirt, page 62.)

Evening Top and Skirt with Yoke
The top, in gold lamé, is fully lined.
The skirt is made from cream shantung.

CHAPTER 10
Flared Skirt

A flared skirt fits at the waist and flares at the hemline with optional amounts of fullness. A picture of this garment appears on page 46.

Diagram 1

Draw in the basic skirt and mark in the lines (refer to diagrams A and B).

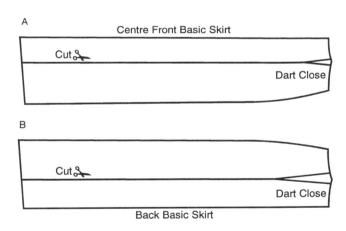

A

Centre Front Basic Skirt

Cut ✄

Dart Close

B

Cut ✄

Dart Close

Back Basic Skirt

Diagram 2

When the darts close, a distance or flare is gained at the hem line (refer to diagrams C and D). This is called pivoting.

Adding 8 cm (3") to centre front and back of your new skirt pattern will allow you to elasticise the waist, creating a simple pull-on.

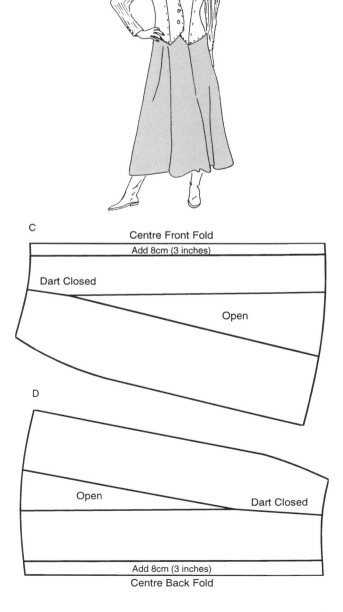

C

Centre Front Fold

Add 8cm (3 inches)

Dart Closed

Open

D

Open

Dart Closed

Add 8cm (3 inches)

Centre Back Fold

CHAPTER 11
Skirt with Yoke

A picture of this garment appears on page 18.

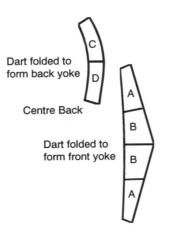

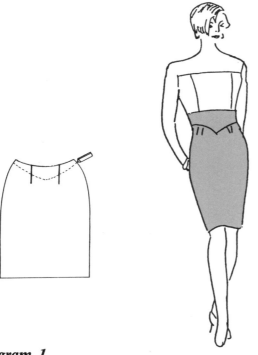

Diagram 1

Draw in lines on your basic skirt pattern. Mark in the lines for the yoke on your calico skirt while you are wearing it.

Diagram 4

The darts on the top part of the skirt will fold out leaving the yoke.

Diagram 2

Transfer the appropriate lines on to your paper skirt pattern. Cut along the lines.

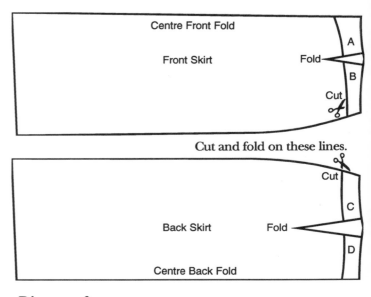

Cut and fold on these lines.

Diagram 3

The darts will form tucks in the front and back skirt.

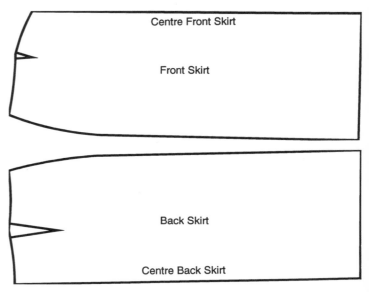

CHAPTER 12
Top with Dolman Sleeves

Once you have your individual block pattern for a bodice you can get some practice in pattern-making! I suggest you make this simple dolman sleeve top. A picture of this garment appears on page 17.

You will not need the back block at all.

Transfer the back neck to the front pattern as shown by the diagram below.

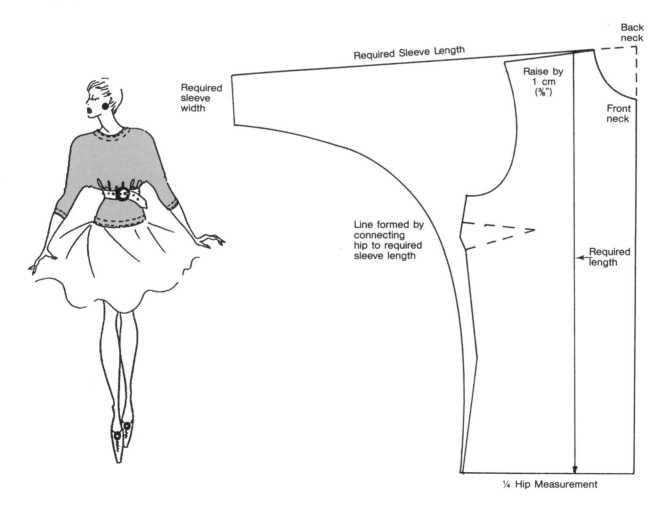

Required Sleeve Length

Required sleeve width

Line formed by connecting hip to required sleeve length

Raise by 1 cm (³⁄₈")

Back neck

Front neck

Required length

¼ Hip Measurement

CHAPTER 13
Sleeveless Top

This sleeveless jacket can be made in all kinds of fabrics, both printed and woven, following the easy directions below. A picture of this garment appears on page 46.

Diagram 1

Mark in your basic front and back blocks. Draw in required design lines.

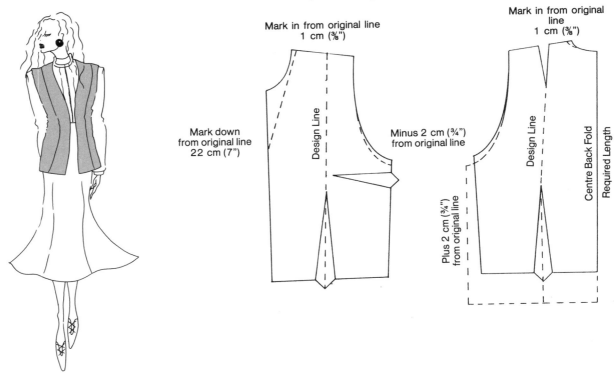

Mark in from original line 1 cm (⅜")

Mark in from original line 1 cm (⅜")

Mark down from original line 22 cm (7")

Design Line

Minus 2 cm (¾") from original line

Design Line

Centre Back Fold

Required Length

Plus 2 cm (¾") from original line

Diagram 2

Cut and pivot your block pattern to create design. Add 2.5 cm (1") to the front for overlap.

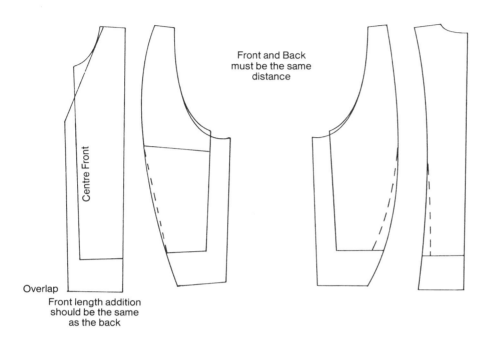

Front and Back must be the same distance

Centre Front

Overlap

Front length addition should be the same as the back

Add seam allowance. Depending on the fabric, this garment can have facings or be fully lined.

CHAPTER 14
Vest

A picture of the vest appears on page 46.

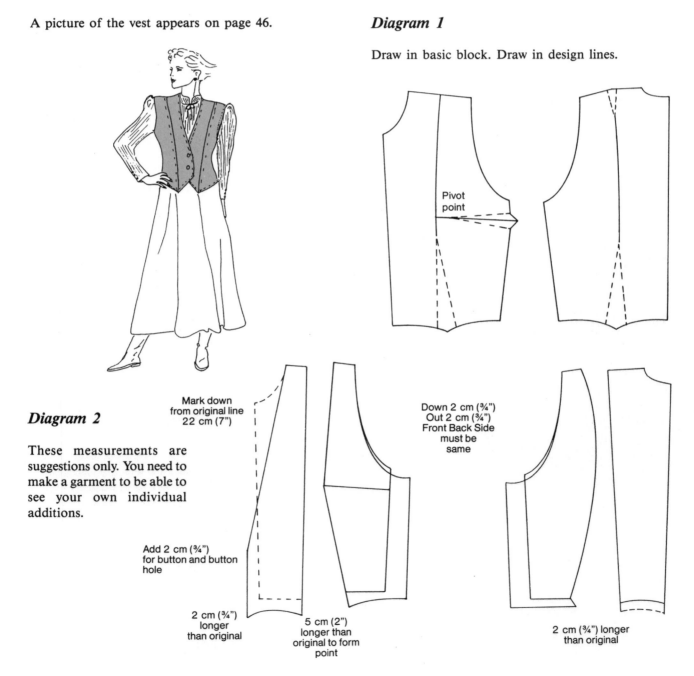

Diagram 1

Draw in basic block. Draw in design lines.

Pivot point

Diagram 2

These measurements are suggestions only. You need to make a garment to be able to see your own individual additions.

Mark down from original line 22 cm (7")

Add 2 cm (¾") for button and button hole

2 cm (¾") longer than original

5 cm (2") longer than original to form point

Down 2 cm (¾")
Out 2 cm (¾")
Front Back Side must be same

2 cm (¾") longer than original

CHAPTER 15
Shirt with Rolled Collar

This shirt has a rolled collar and pleated front and shoulders. The opening on the right shoulder is trimmed with several buttons. Adding a seam at the centre front and a Chinese collar will create the shirt on page 45.

Diagram 2

Measure the length required for your sleeve.

Diagram 3

Following the diagram on page 56, draw in required sleeve length.

Diagram 1

Draw in your basic block patterns. Add alterations as shown in the diagrams below. Extending the side seam past the bust dart will eliminate the bust dart.

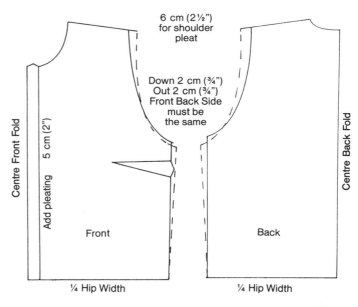

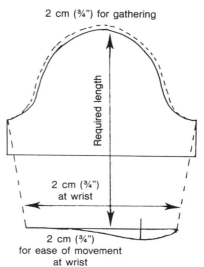

71

Diagram 4

The sleeve can be narrowed or widened at the cuff for a more fitted effect.

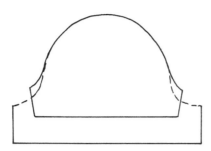

Diagram 5

To form a space for a placket, measure the sleeve at the wrist. Halve this measurement, then halve it again and mark this point at the back of the sleeve. Draw a vertical line 5 cm (2") long. This is the placket. The sleeve hem has to be lowered by 2 cm (¾") at this point and reshaped in an S curve.

Diagram 6

To make a cuff pattern, first measure your wrist.

Draw a rectangle the length of your wrist measurement, adding 2.5 cm (1") at each end; the width should be 5 cm (2") for a single button cuff and 10 cm (4") for a two button cuff.

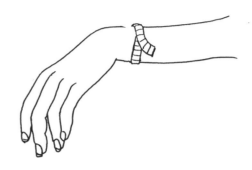

Add seam allowances in the fabric but *not* in the interlining.

Note   Skirt waistbands are made in the same manner.

CHAPTER 16
Shirt Dress

This shirt dress can be made to any length you wish. A picture appears on page 28.

1. Mark in your basic front and back bodice on the pattern paper.
2. Draw in yoke for front and back.
3. Add 2.5 cm (1") at the centre back for extra fullness.

4. Add centre front swing (see page 40, Diagram 12). Then add 2 cm (¾") for button and buttonholes.
5. Drop armholes by 2 cm (¾").
6. Extend under front and back armhole by 2 cm (¾").
7. Add the required length.
8. Cut and separate the front and back yoke.
9. Fold the dart out from the back yoke.
10. Pivot the bust dart. This will give you the pleat at the chest.

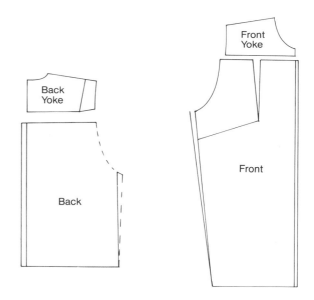

11. Drop sleeve and add 2 cm (¾") at front and back armhole. Adjust for sleeve length.
12. For the collar use the shirt collar from page 57.

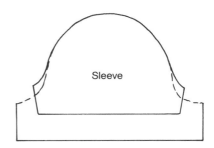

CHAPTER 17
Evening Top

The pattern for this sleeveless fitted top can be made by adapting your calico top. A picture of it appears on page 64.

1. Draw the design on your calico top while you are wearing it.
2. Transfer the marks from your calico top to the paper pattern.

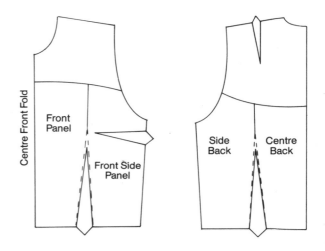

3. Pivot the front darts following the method explained on page 49 in Chapter 5.
4. Separate the front into two separate pieces forming the front and side panels.

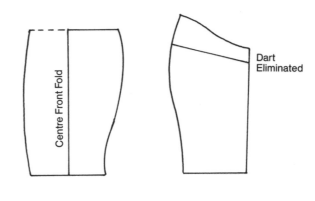

5. Eliminate the back dart by folding it out.

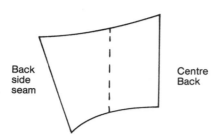

CHAPTER 18
Sewing and Construction Tips

With practice, and using the drafting methods outlined in this book, you should be able quickly to make garments for yourself and your family—adults, children, babies, even dolls. Remember to adjust for different neck sizes and shoulder slopes.

During my thirty years of sewing commercially and teaching and listening to dressmakers I have compiled a few important sewing hints.

Diagram 1

The simplest way to find out how much fabric you should buy is to:

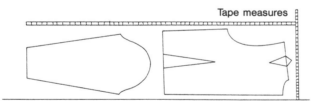

1. Lay a tape measure at right angles to the edge of your carpet.
2. Decide what width of fabric you would like to buy and place a second tape measure at this distance parallel to the edge of the carpet.
3. Place all your pattern pieces in the space between the tape measure and the edge of the carpet.

With this method you should be able to tell at a glance the right width; the other tape will show you the required length.

As a general rule you will need twice your skirt, slacks or dress length in metric 90 cm or 115 cm fabric (imperial 36" or 45"). If your material is metric 150 cm (imperial 60") you need once your skirt, slacks or dress length. The sleeve is once the length you require regardless of fabric width.

Diagram 2

Before you start to cut out your pattern, press all pattern pieces, then measure and check.

1. Does the neck balance?

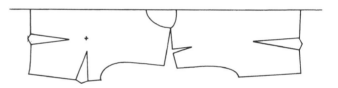

2. Are the shoulders and side seams even? If the garment has a collar, does it fit? Is the sleeve the right measurement for the armhole? Literally make up your garment and check the measurements for bust, shoulder to waist and length. Use the earlier chapters of this book for reference on how to do this.

   If you take time and do this before cutting your fabric you will save a lot of time and frustration. Do not trust any pattern. They can contain errors. My main rule is: *I can always fix the paper pattern, it is only paper.* Material is expensive and very hard to fix once it is wrongly cut.

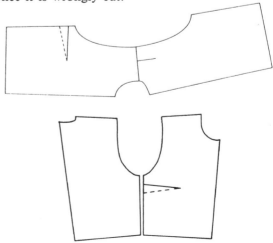

Diagram 3

After the fabric and any interfacing is cut I always start by attaching the interfacing to the collar, cuffs or pockets by sewing or pressing. It is a good idea to have a minimal or no seam allowance on the interfacing. This helps to eliminate bulk in the finished garment.

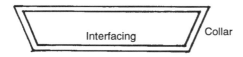

Diagram 4

Always trim the corners of collars and cuffs (see the diagram), then turn to the correct side, press and have them ready to assemble.

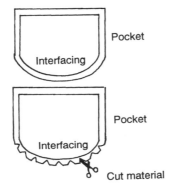

Diagram 5

Your next move is to start sewing the darts in the garment. If the garment has panels, they come next. Then the shoulder seams—now press this seam. In fact, have an iron ready and press every seam as soon as you sew it. This is the difference between a professional and an amateur finish.

Why?
1. The curves must be cut. See diagrams. If the garment on the ironing board is not lying flat, it will look the same on you. Ironing should tell you if you have to cut the fabric in more deeply or not.
2. Ironing a seam shows if it has been stretched or eased. If this is the case, it should be redone at this point rather than finding it out when the garment is finished.
3. When the seams are ironed it will be easier to see that the seam at the waist is facing the same way it is at the hem.
4. Sew on the collar or facings. *Press*. Next sew the side seams.

Cutting curves

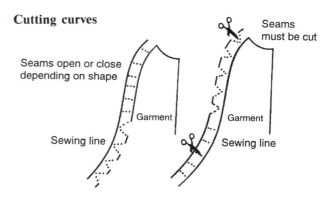

Ironing seams

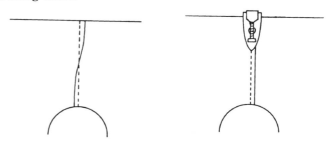

Diagram 6

1. If the garment has a sleeve, make it up now. There should be a gathering stitch at the head of the sleeve, which will help you with sewing it in.

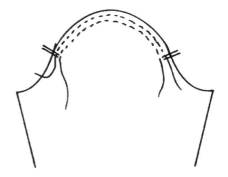

2. Always sew sleeve in with the gathered side uppermost. Use a pin to help divide the material evenly as you sew it in the armhole.

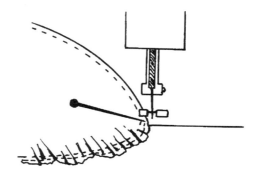

Diagram 7

Don't ever sew a fitted sleeve in before the side seam is closed. The sleeve will pull and disfigure the garment, which will also inhibit your arm movement. The only time it is okay to do this is when the armhole is very loose, e.g. a dolman sleeve.

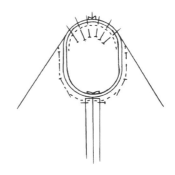

Diagram 8
BUTTONHOLES

Erasable pens are wonderful for buttonholes. Just draw in the marks and you will get accuracy with the most basic sewing machines.

Diagram 9

The garment should always be tried on for length before the hem is taken up. The most ingenious way I have seen a hemline marked is by getting a piece of cotton, rubbing it with chalk, then tying the cotton between two chairs at the height required. See diagram. Wearing your garment, turn around slowly, pressing against the cotton. The chalk will mark your hemline.

Pressing a hem before sewing it will give you the desired finish.

Author's Note

I have covered the basic block in this book, and am planning future publications which will show how the basic block can be altered for individual designing and to give advice on figure faults and how to overcome them.

If you have any queries or are interested in further instructions, you can contact me, enclosing a self-addressed envelope, at P.O. Box 52, Jannali NSW 2226.

Basic Course Outline

The book *Magic Drafting* has been specifically written and set out as a step by step self-help book. Magic Drafting courses are currently being taught in schools and colleges using this book in the format set out below. There are also correspondence and hands-on courses available if you would like to take the opportunity of doing them. Courses are held at Bondi and Parramatta and through correspondence. Contact Magic Drafting, P.O. Box 52, Jannali NSW 2226.

Course outline

Lesson 1

Activity
- Reading this book and following the instructions on skirts.
- Create a gored skirt.

Outcome
- At the end of this lesson the student will be able to:
  - ☐ Measure an individual body shape to create a skirt pattern.
  - ☐ Demonstrate the ability to create different types of gored skirts.

Lesson 2

Activity
- Fitting a straight skirt, creating darts and waist line.
- Designing A-line skirts and skirts with a yoke insert.

Outcome
- At the end of this lesson the student will be able to:
  - ☐ Create a well fitting tailored skirt, no longer depending on a commercial pattern for a skirt design.

Lesson 3

Activity
- From this book, read and follow instructions for bodice.
- Cut and fit bodice in calico.
- Create a perfect fitting bodice block.

Outcome
- At the end of this lesson the student will be able to:
  - ☐ Describe why patterns have not fitted in the past.
  - ☐ Demonstrate the relationship between art and mathematics (in regard to pattern-making) by making a bodice block.
  - ☐ Create patterns for the individual.

Lesson 4

Activity
- From this book follow and create a sleeve pattern.
- Design a simple top.

Outcome
- At the end of this lesson the student will be able to:
  - ☐ Demonstrate how to change and interpret designs.
  - ☐ Display the work skill to create a design for an individual body and taste.

Lesson 5

Activity
- From this book, design a collar.
- Design another top of your choice.

Outcome
- At the end of this lesson the student will be able to:
  - ☐ Make a design from a picture in a magazine or create one from your own imagination.
  - ☐ Show a new and different outlook on pattern-making and practical use in time management.

Drafting Supplies

Materials required for drafting can be ordered through Magic Drafting, P.O. Box 52, Jannali NSW 2226. (All prices in Australian dollars.)

1. **Ruler** $20.00
   5 cm (2") wide—fully transparent, fully flexible

2. **Magic marking pen** $15.00
   Erases in 24 hours, guaranteed not to mark white silk

3. **Magnetic tray** $8.00
   Great sewing accessory

4. **Tracing wheel** (industrial) $15.00
   Razor sharp pin points—transfers through any fabric onto paper—no damage to fabric

5. **Pattern paper** (brown) $5.00
   112 cm wide with lines, approx. 4 m

6. **Books** *(Magic Drafting)* $14.95
   Each planned title will contain step by step instructions for a range of specific garments

7. **Video** *(Magic Drafting)* $30.00
   How to alter your paper patterns. How to use the ruler and excerpts from the *Magic Drafting* book.

8. **One Day Course** (Slacks) $100.00
   Start in the morning, leave with perfect fitting pants for you and any friends or relations.

9. **One Day Course** (Dress) $60.00
   Bring your paper patterns, learn how to achieve a perfect fitting garment to your own individual taste.

10. **Basic Beginner Course** $300.00
    Learn to do all types of skirts and a top of your own design plus collars and sleeves.

11. **Advanced Course or Per Each Lesson** $50.00
    Using your individual block you will create to any design any perfect fitting garment of your choice.

12. **Membership** (Club) $50.00
    Club members will receive a newsletter and can write to Gabriella for advice, problems and supplies.

Magic Drafting Order Form

Name:					
Address:					
Postcode:				Phone:	
Items		Price	Items		Price
1			7		
2			8		
3			9		
4			10		
5			11		
6			12		

PLEASE COMPLETE THE ORDER FORM AND POST CHEQUE OR MONEY ORDER TO
MAGIC DRAFTING, PO BOX 52, JANNALI NSW 2226, SYDNEY AUSTRALIA
(ADD $00.00 EXTRA FOR PACKING, POSTAGE AND DELIVERY

INDEX